I believe in love at first sight. The manuscript falls open to "Bray," and I know I am in the presence of an original, gorgeous, lyric voice. By the time I reach "The Kiss," I am hopelessly smitten by Ellen Rowland and *No Small Thing*. Get a copy for yourself and another for someone you love.

Donna Hilbert
author of *Threnody*

By turns ekphrastic, ecstatic, and experiential, Ellen Rowland's *No Small Thing* is rich with sensory and sensuous gifts, like all the earth's fruits. I love how these attentive poems bring the faraway nearby and allow us to witness beauty, love, and grace as Rowland does, up close and personal.

Michael Kleber-Diggs
author of *Worldly Things*

In Ellen Rowland's *No Small Thing* I find I am learning how to love again, how to slow down, how to live. She reminds me, as I needed to be reminded: "You are unique only in your brokenness." The wisdom of these poems is deep, and they bring us to the senses again and again: the sweetness of papaya, the bird sounds of loved ones waking up, sounds of coffee percolating. As I read this collection, I find I am re-seeing my own life with a refreshed and enlivened perspective. I feel quieted and restored, like a gentle yoga class, stretched in just the right places.

Laura Foley
winner of the Common Good Books Poetry Contest

Ellen Rowland's words distill the aching beauty of presence. They let us "swim among weightless / stars" and "consider the cosmos / beneath our feet." In this slim volume, the inexpressible finds its way to us through a "network of roots," "tender tomatoes rouging in morning sun," and "silence lush with listening." *No Small Thing* is a boundless wonder.

Laura Grace Weldon
2019 Ohio Poet of the Year

No Small Thing

Poems

Ellen Rowland

Fernwood
PRESS

No Small Thing

©2023 by Ellen Rowland

Fernwood Press
Newberg, Oregon
www.fernwoodpress.com

Printed in the United States of America

Cover and page design: Mareesa Fawver Moss
Author photo: Sunny Rowland

ISBN 978-1-59498-109-8

*In memory of my mother
Rosemary Ford Lanahan*

and for Richard, Jamie, and Sunny

Table of Contents

Introduction by James Crews

Reading through Ellen Rowland's newest book, *No Small Thing*, I shook my head and smiled as I finished each poem with relish, then went back to read it again. It is exceedingly rare to find a poet whose every work seems to slice the world into accessible and wondrous portions, much like the beetroot she describes early on in the collection— "silky red velvet" that "slips onto the white plate." When I work with beginning poets, I often have to convince them of the pleasures of writing from the senses, using the actual, physical world to bring readers more deeply into a scene. In Ellen's poems, however, you will find every one of your senses awakened, as she lovingly recreates each moment, whether describing a donkey's bray or capturing the bittersweet sight of her daughter getting ready in the morning, tying her hair back and walking out the door.

These poems also open up what Jane Hirshfield has called "window-moments," allowing the imagination to diverge in surprising ways from the initial image or inspiration. In "The Story in Me Is Red," for instance, what begins as a meditation on the blood that fills us all soon reveals that the story inside each of us is, in truth, wild and uncontainable:

> The story in me wants to be
> a horse in freedom,
> an eagle hunting, a cloud forming,
> a worm churning nutrients
> that feed the rich
> layers of all stories.

Such masterful reaching beyond one's beginning subject shows us a writer at the height of her powers. In "This Body," the simple sight of purple fodder vetch "sprung up overnight in the garden" becomes an exploration of her own physical transformations over the years, until she asks the essential question of herself: "When did I stop celebrating the evolution of me?" After that, we find her suddenly in love with herself again: "I slick my lips with gloss, slip on a smile, a shawl," she says, briefly shedding the roles of wife and mother.

More than anything else, a wide-open embrace of life flavors these poems as she savors the ups and downs, the joys and losses that often coexist. In one of the most exquisite poems in the book, "What Branches Hold," she asks: "Did you/ever think you could be so lost and so found/ in the same visible breath?" So often we move through our lives dissatisfied with ourselves and our bodies, believing a better moment awaits us in some nonexistent future. Yet Ellen Rowland's grounded poems capture the fullness of being human, along with the redemption found in deep presence and the giving of our attention—which is, as her title rightfully points out, "no small thing." Each poem urges us to see, as the great farmer-poet Wendell Berry once put it: "What we need is here."

—James Crews
author of *Kindness Will Save the World*
and editor of *The Wonder of Small Things*

The Way the Sky Might Taste

The bite of a softened cardamom pod
in a spoonful of Tikka Masala.
Tang of copper, caperberry,
other berries too:
a rasp, a blue, a lingon, elder
lit zest of lemon, thin slice of moon.
The breath of a first kiss,
sweet and deeply surprising.
Dirt on the youngest tongue, the red
flesh of a torn fig eaten
straight from the tree,
the constellation of wings
as champagne leaves the flute.

A Memory of Kerala

I bought a bowl of fresh fruit on the mid-day
beach of Kovalam from an old, fleshy woman
who wore the colors of her fruit—soft
papaya undershirt patterned with shiny black
pearls the size of passion seeds. Sari a glistening mango
sheath folded to reveal the outer green skin,
white coconut sap woven with silk husks
draped over one shoulder. She bent over her bowl
and expertly carved the fruit, spraying happy
gnats about her face, then wiped her blade
on a pulpy rag. I poured coins (a deceivingly full fist
of rupee) into her sticky palm and went to sit
under an umbrella next to a woman
in a hot-pink yoga bra who cautioned me
not to eat it. I would surely be sick, she said.
Something about the heat and bacteria
and that Indian woman being unwashed.
I took my fruit and stood in the serried waves
and ate it anyway, fingers to mouth, juice
down the chin, cool and ripe and reckless,
tasting just like the otherness I had come for.

Dervish

Pulse with the bloodbeat,
as humankind turns on itself.
Revolve around the silent heart,
lamenting the ego's rise.
Whirl against the tenor of fear
deafening love's right to be heard.
Spin a careful nautilus
to float the stranger to shore.
Embrace the tripping differences
shrouded by skin and veil.
Twirl and thrash in endless tears
to the bliss of a borderless dance.
We are hidden beneath your flowing folds.
Dissolve us into One.

Gravity

Turn the world upside down
so that I might swim among weightless
stars, bathe in tidal pools of cool
blue nothingness, song of sky
stretched past Source,
a shimmer of something
grander than hope, brighter than self.

May I look up then
and contemplate the endless green
of sprouting trees,
hands linked together stitching borders,
whole oceans of love.
Galaxy upon galaxy of kindness
pulling me back.

Heart Beet

I slice into the silky red velvet
of a steamed beetroot
and a warm
paper-thin heart
slips onto the white plate—
the perfect shape and stain,
matte and veined
like a river map
of life's coils and turns.
I serve you the tender omen
as though the soil has stamped
a woodcut of our years together
and offered us the shape
of another twenty.

The Kiss

Before we were we,
I would study
your lips as you spoke, longing
to be a single word formed there and said.
Your top lip stimulated
my intellect (you had so much to say)
while the bottom stirred up instinct:
breath and whispers,
slick sliding and buttery biting.
I cooked for you
just to watch you eat. Imagined myself
the fork, the salt, the meat
passing under your soft palate
and resting there in warmth.
When you finally offered me
your mouth, everything
became you,
and I feasted there,
wild and fed.

Marriage Tanka

I'll never ask you
for more than you can give me.
I'll lasso the moon
myself, hitch a ride on light,
send you back fistfuls of stars.

Morning Tanka

I wake to your need
rising lightly under me.
Oh, the breath of us
holding under light cotton,
letting go, a death of sorts.

Birds Call the News to Each Other

as I steal a few more minutes
of warmth against your back

       Sun is here, cold, cold gone

we are already in different worlds
as I pull the covers aside, dress quickly

       As you are, come sun, gold

layer tinder and kindling in the woodstove,
fists of paper propping

       Berries bright, there a thread, bring

the smaller twigs as they chat and catch
to light the larger logs

       Quickly now, quickly home, tree

all quiet but the drip, drip, shhh of coffee
steam tendrils, aroma cloud, cold stone floor

       Join me now, warm warm, we

hosting a patch of sun I go stand in
as I wait for our bread to toast

       Glory day, glory day, see?

The Gift

For no particular reason,
not her birthday,
their anniversary,
or Mother's Day,
he gives her a bronze buddha
the size of a large pear. The buddha
holds a cast lotus flower,
the lotus flower holds a votive
that when lit gives off
the smell of pine needles
crushed under feet
searching for a quiet moment
in the forest. The forest holds the world
it seems, ferns and lichen, mossy patches
and deep, damp roots. The network of roots anchors
the canopy of trees overhead, home to
nests and cocoons and other wombs. She brings
both her hands to her own instinctively
forming a bowl, her offering. Startled
by nuzzled leaves, she stands stock still
in the calm and awful presence of a deer,
antlers like a floating chandelier.
Both their hearts pulse like small flames
near breath. And she thinks
how well he knows her.

Imperfect Buddha Haibun

You are unique only in your brokenness, your numerous decapitations a seamed necklace of attempted repairs. There is a perfect one of you somewhere in a store that holds no meaning for me. I find your flaws familiar and comforting, top petal re-glued, right lotus edge missing, chips exposing the casting of your make. And yet, you sit so serenely, so at peace with all your imperfections. Aren't we asked daily to love things as they are? To notice, then tenderly accept the faults of others? Of ourselves? You offer me with no shame this lesson deep in the cracks

don't try to fix me
my brokenness holds beauty
this is how to love

Bird

She lay there still
and perfect
quiet heart and cold feathers
feet like tiny branches in
my hands, a final home.
She must have met her own
reflection in the pane
mistaking it for
a potential nestmate.
A comforting thought
that her quick death was
framed in such joyful
abandon.
She wouldn't
have hesitated
crashing without thinking
into the rush of another
unlike most humans who hover
far too long, fearing what might
break, craving something softer,
something easy, wanting only
to coast on cloudless light.

Bray

Yesterday I heard a donkey bray,
the loud staccato bellow rising from
the belly like a frightened choke.
And then such a deep retch of sorrow
that another answered in mimic.
In the bray, I thought I recognized
the grasp of
abandonment or eternal solitude
or loneliness, plain and simple. And I
wanted to open my ribs and lungs and
release the same cry, but instead
I found the donkey, tethered to a tree,
standing in the circle of his own grazing,
and I told him he was beautiful
and loved.

A Satisfied Citizen of Your Own Life

Imagine a life spent loving what is already good,
stopping to give thanks to the thermos
that keeps your morning coffee warm
and your hands, too, when you wrap them
with an outbreath around the smooth cylinder.

Pausing, as you wash each fork and knife, to remember those
who sat at your table the night before, noticing which friend
discreetly hid the chanterelles under a lettuce leaf
so that next time, you'll stop trying so hard to impress,
make an omelet instead.

Considering, as suds dissolve fingerprints
on clouded glasses that still hold
the ruby dregs of a gifted Merlot,
the joyous news of someone's cancer remission
still in the air like a song you can't get out of your head.

Imagine also the tender tomatoes rouging in morning sun
that you will whisper to and pick as soon as steaming
water flowing from working pipes washes you clean
of yesterday's assumptions, leaving you naked and awake
to what you might do with this day, what small
kindness you might offer, who you might take in your arms
and love.

Daughter

No words but not silent either
the stretch and snap of elastic as your wrists
tie your tangled morning hair,
feet drumming the floor with dream-heavy purpose,
your latest favorite song sleep hummed.
You come into view, and I wonder who you are,
when we became separated, cleaved in two,
what private life you live, what loves and fears
and worries occupy your thoughts. Or maybe I am
assigning too much to your growing heart. Maybe
all you want is breakfast before stepping into flipflops,
a fig in your hand on the way to meet friends
at the beach. A quick peck on the cheek,
and your morning smell goes out the door.
Once, many years ago, I lost sight of
you in the grocery store. You simply toddled away.

Birth Story

A reminder after all these years
twice opened like a love letter
the scar reddens to be heard,
a phantom pain tugging
at seventeen years
of cutting chords.
I touch it
lightly
once.
This
is me.
I am scarred.
I share the knife,
tell you the story
of how we were both born,
opened up to each other
on a bright day in early May
that comes round and around, told again.

I Dreamt of Milk Sloshing in Pails

milk seeping
through cracked porcelain bowls,
which made me think
of thinned white paint
spilling, impossible
to clean or of losing something
precious, like water
through cupped palms.
What is the message?
Be careful
with the paint tray?
Don't cry over spilt milk?
Something about motherhood,
my inability to breastfeed
still nagging my subconscious.
Always interesting
to consider the stuff
of dreams.
In this case, maybe it's just
a simple reminder to myself
to buy a carton
for the kid's cereal.
I am low again. In my own way,
I am still providing milk,
and so it goes on the list.

Lullaby

(after Leslie Marmon Silko)

Sleep,
sleep.
You are one with the world.
The mountain is your mother,
she rocks you gently.
The forest is your father,
he sings to you softly.
Rest,
rest.
Fern is your sister,
she shades you selflessly.
Rain and sun are your brothers,
they nourish you endlessly.
Dream,
dream.
You are one with earth.
There was never a time
when you
were not loved.

Poetry Ancestors

(with thanks to Joy Harjo)

The poet said *Breath will take you to the story.*
Everything in between is worth holding.
She offered relics, broken history, broken clay.
What the ancestors have to say is all there on the map
of your story. Ask, then listen. Listen
to memory, speak to the sacred. The words
that go sideways will slip in.
What's overheard in dreams,
on subways, lines from dog-eared pages
are your generous forefathers and grandmothers
of this writing now. Sing your way through
the poems that recognize something in you.
Commit them to memory, borrow their knowing.
What is the animal that speaks to you?
Write its body down in the
notebook you carry.

She had some horses. She had some horses.

The rhythm moved me to this permission
to catch her horses, speak to them softly,
let them run through a poem
of my own making. Not stolen horses,
red cliff horses who waited for resurrection,
kept safe in hidden pockets, sewn into seams,
close by on the bedside table.

Placed on the tongue nightly,
not from hunger but from a love of
language that binds our cavernous wounds
and tames us with its speaking.

The Faraway Nearby

(with thoughts of Georgia O'Keeffe)

I thought the desert would feel lonely at night.
There was life just beyond, I knew,
although at first all I could see
was a mesa of darkness
against which played the scorching day.

Negative space of heat in relief, walking
fragments of bleached bone and callous clay,
meeting the improbable flower here and there.
How far down had its roots reached
to find the last vein of humid earth?
And why was it so insistent on blooming?

I saw there or felt or imagined—
eyes adjusting to the parched wide night—
both animal presence and the dance
of generations circling a fragile bonfire.
Ashes now tamped, bones now cold,
voices evaporated, absorbed by the stem
of a Mariposa Lily.

I felt my smallness then in that bowl of sky
so full of pinpoint light. I was not alone
in what I knew. That we are all held
by an infinite constellation, an eddy of stories
kept bright in the telling.

The Story in Me Is Red

Not the red of anger
but the red of urgency,
of river moving
through me.

The story in me
renews itself daily
as blood circulating.
I wake with the same bones,
but some new version
has come to live in me, nesting
then just as soon poised to fly,
to land near you
and you and you.

The story in me wants to be
a horse in freedom,
an eagle hunting, a cloud forming,
a worm churning nutrients
that feed the rich
layers of all stories.

All I ever ask of the story in me
is to leave gently, to sing
in the voice I gave it.

Self Love

For you, I will ride a bike downhill
and ring the bell, the *bring, bring, bring*
of my passing. I will use voice and bell. *I am here.*
I will eat unshy spoonfuls of ice cream, cold
shameless sliding, tongue searching pecans,
rummy raisins, peppery vanilla seeds. I will
pick yellow flowers and put them in a blue vase, light
a candle. For you, I will never again say
How stupid. You don't deserve this. That will never fit.
I will bite my habit tongue and fashion a new language,
a whole lexicon of kindness.
They say you can rewire the brain
with gentle acts and words. I will wrap
every synapse in my arms and whisper
the neversaids until they fire off harder truths to hear
like *you are loved* and *don't you look beautiful today.*

With Age

I sometimes long to be free
from my role as wife and mother,
from my responsibility to others,
from my hard inner critic,
from the mirror, from the mat.

I long to know things, unnameable,
that only the soul can sense
without the mind interfering. The simple
things the heart knows. And, please,
I long to be free of worries and pain and fear.

I long to make bread all day or
contemplate the fire in the hearth
or stare into nothingness
without someone asking,
"Are you okay?"

I long to write from the very well
of me without a shadow of ego
until ink and words run out.
I long for a day with no notifications,
no clocks, no chores, no calls.

I crave the silence of an endless walk
where I don't have to use language,
trees and birds and insects of wonder
just being with me in the world
without needing my words.

I long to eat a pear or a fig with
my eyes closed, tasting the thunder, the rain,
the breath of a busy wasp. Then to sit
in a too hot bath until the feel of air
and water on skin meet and become one.

At the end of the day, I long to
sleep on both sides of the bed
and wrap myself in the covers
until I am reborn. Funny how my
younger self would have called this
being lonely.

This Body

I wish I could look upon this body
with the same wonder I offer to the purple fodder vetch
sprung up overnight in the garden. Sweet indecency,
their sheaths flirt shamelessly with honeybees. When
was the last time I dressed myself to attract anything?
Everything changes. There is nothing to fix
but the desire to fix. My once dark mane is now a skein of silver,
my stomach a swollen womb in menopause. But, oh,
how it all worked. Works still.

When did I stop celebrating the evolution of me?

I slick my lips with gloss, slip on a smile, a shawl.
Move through the not yet morning grass, run my fingers
over a damp patch of moss, hum a little
for no one.

Trip

A stupid fall, you will say.
Nothing daring or graceful, just a trip
on something insignificant and small while having
successfully avoided the lip of a flat stone
or a protruding root on this same
path for months now. You will scan
your body, noticing where the heat rises
to throb the grated skin, the swelling shin,
the throbbing elbow. You will blow
dirt and grit from the palms of
the hands that braced you, the cool air
of your breath soothing the sting.

You will not hop back up as you once could
but sit or lay with your vulnerability,
this further proof of impermanence,
and give thanks, deep gratitude
as you circle wrists, ankles, neck,
that most of you is still in good working order.

On the way home, you will conjure
the names of each bone and tendon spared
with no understanding of when or how
you acquired the knowledge.

No Small Thing

The smell of baking bread, smooth floured hands,
butter waiting to be spread with blackberry jam,
and I realize, this is no small thing.
These days spent confined,
I am drawn to life's ordinary details,
the largeness of all we can do
alongside what we cannot.
The list of allowances far outweighs my complaints.
I am fortunate to have flour and yeast, a source of heat,
not to mention soft butter, the tartness of blackberries
harvested on a cold back road.
A kitchen, a home, two working
hands to stir and knead,
a clear enough head to gather it all.
Even the big toothy knife feels miraculous
as it grabs hold and cracks the crust.

What Remains

I am absent
always with you
hidden in your pocket as a note on pulpy paper.
In your hair as the gentle pull of comb.
I am the jazz tune that plays on repeat,
the kitchen towel thrown over one shoulder.
A fingerprint on the recipe card, raised with years
of dried flour and butter. Run your finger
over the braille of me and know I flow
in you as cell and sugar. The final breakdown
of me will scatter with the wind, burrow deep
with the earthworm, migrate in beaks
to far away soil as seed and source and song.
I am everywhere, letting go, holding on.

When the World Was Whole

did it not hold us all together
in one great bowl? Feather, bone,
leaf, gill, and cloud. Atoms
were atoms, tongues tongues,
skin skin. Land sprawled
without claim.

Waters fed each other.
We led to each other.

Hallelujahs were sent up for small
bowls of rice with broth, for fresh bread
baked by clay, clay baked by sun.
For abundant crops, for birth and another
year lived, we offered *merci* and *mashallah*.
Dance and song lifted skyward the day
the rains came here, the day the rains stopped there.

Seams were made in old soles that wore
a path to the water hole that gave and gave
without complaint. Cloth was sewn together turning
three tattered robes into one brightly colored cloak.
We praised the needle, the thread, the eye,
the nimble hand, the old wearer who held
knowledge of which plants healed what wounds.

The echo of all that simple praise lives on
in each thing we hold up to the light. Don't tell me
you don't hear it when you put down your phone,
in the quiet bow of your head when you're alone,
it settles into the hollow just behind your breast,
lives in between the want of your pressed palms.
When day comes home and you sit across from love,
the table spread with enough for everyone, with enough,
you think to yourself, maybe even say out loud,
Thank you, thank you, thank you.

I Start This Day

with a green breath of consequence
inhaling the green, green grass blades,
dew soaked soil underfoot grounding,
taking in the growth, the holy imperfections
of our un-chemicaled good intentions.
Worm holed heads of curly lettuce—
each like an elegant celadon dressing gown,
amethyst beetroot veins running up red reaching leaves,
basil in an unremarkable pot by the door.
Tomato buds already smelling like
the Caprese salad we'll eat in early July
when I'll remember with precision
this slow solitary parade.

Dandelions in November

Ropes of yellow clarity parade the charring field.
Sweet, stubborn cogs of summer
just beginning to curl in on themselves, limp
leaves no longer fit for salad.
I pick one small sun
and pop it in my mouth, incredulous
that I am able to hold light and earth
and bee work on my tongue.

Noticing: A Burning Haibun

I.

Gray doves alight in knowing pairs
in the branch above my quiet morning.
Goat bells—this one a dull tong, that one
a high ting—chime the early path
of grazing, displacing bees lazed by dew.
Truck and tractor crawl, good farmer calls
to good farmer "good day" as gears begin to shift.
Neighbor in a turquoise dress walks her small white
dog, startling Swallows in the tree, a fluttered V
that takes me higher than I ever intended. Right up
to a wide, waking sky that grows my world. Such
gratitude for what I thought was silence. For what I
thought was solitude.

II.

Knowing pairs
my quiet morning,
a dull tong
the early path
to "good day."
A turquoise tree,
a fluttered V,
a wide waking gratitude
was silence,
was solitude.

III.

Knowing pairs the path,
a turquoise tree, fluttered V,
waking gratitude

Gratitude List

(after Laura Foley)

Praise be this morning for dawning gray,
the cool respite, the cottoned sea,
a light shawl pulled from the box marked "fall."
Praise be the silent sleepers
undisturbed by aging ankles, bare feet beneath
my cotton gown, picking up pale threads and
salty sand as I cross the floor.
Praise be the paint peeled door, closing
silently behind, the cat slipping through
just in time. Praise be the smell of slow
pressed coffee, the yawn of the pour,
the flea market mug from a lifetime ago.
Praise be the warmth in my grateful hands,
the hour before me, the white page, the pen.

Crooked Hallelujah*

And I, too, have prayed
in my own way
with my fellow parishioners in this old-growth nave
where knots and burl transform
into faces I commit to memory. Branches become hands
to hold; tender bark to run my fingers over
as fresh wounds form scars
like yours and mine, no less beautiful,
no less true.

So much life in the underbelly
of one lone tree fallen
as a bench for me
and shelter too for the clearcut homeless—
the orphans, the beggars, the newborn, the blind—
all taken in,
feeding each other songs under warm moss.

Fall has come, and I feel the cold need
to press my knees upon this
bed of fallen leaves, kneel in the loamy decay of
ancestors renewing life (already!) in rich layers of
sacrifice.

Here, messages run through the forest floor
in a language we might learn. An unseen mass of roots
whispers together a coda of love
that, if I listen carefully says,
I'll take care of you. You are not alone.
My nutrients are your nutrients.
My soil is your soil.
My sun, your sun.
My soul, your soul.
Your death, my death.
This renewal, our renewal!

How, then, could I not graft my lungs
to the nearest branch and sing out?
A crooked *Hallelujah*
lifted through the understory,
skyward.

*Title borrowed from the book of the same title by Kelli Jo Ford

Migration

The bee eaters are leaving as the sun shortens
making one last swoop across the browning field.
Iridescent blue bellies stun me.

The silent stroke of their languaged wings
carries tender longing for drumming lands.
The bee eaters are leaving as the sun shortens.

Past sea and oak and open gate
I would soar if I could and close the loop
making one last swoop of the browning field.

I will settle for the robin's song.
Let light travel, I will hold its place.
Iridescent blue bellies stun me.

Transformation

after José A. Alcántara

My
wet wings
spread, tracing
infinity.
I hardly miss my
brutish legs, once dull throat.
Mouth of this joyful turning
now a beak of song, longing to
spill forth like a belch of bright rubies

What Branches Hold

This is the hush you've been seeking,
isn't it? Silence lush with listening.
Yes, it's cold, so cold and so?
Haven't you come dressed just for this?
And so you pull the soft wool closer, push
the fleeced collar higher, part
the snow-laden branches
and step in, knowing full well
you will be baptized. Allow yourself
to be called deeper and deeper
into this dense huddle
of gentle bark and quiet drape. Did you
ever think you could be so lost and so found
in the same visible breath?

Frosted Leaves

The Artist
dipped his brush
into the breath
of winter and feathered
blades of dormancy,
leaves brindled silver by
the absence of pigment,
just to remind us
of the tilting axis
we live on.

Rose Worthy

What does it mean to stop
and smell a rose?
First, you have to get out
of your head, your ego mind,
and look around with your real eyes,
your seeing eyes,
not the film that's running an encore
of everything you've done or haven't done
or what you should have said to so and so.
Then you have to stop on your way to
wherever it is you are rushing
and feel, really know, that the rose
is worthy of your time.
Bend down to her. She may be below you,
but she is not beneath you.
She senses this.
Now take her stem between your fingers,
careful not to thorn yourself,
and bring your nose to her blossoms. Inhale.
Her scent will make you close your eyes
as involuntarily as a sneeze.
Then you will know why you stopped
and wonder why you haven't stopped
before and promise to stop again.
Tomorrow and again until her petals begin
to fall around her in a series of small losses.
This is her lifetime. Did you notice?

Adsum

The old pond—
a frog jumps in,
*   sound of water.*   —*Matsuo Basho*

I am here
at the mouth of a small waterfall
sitting on a large stone
pocked by history
and veined by rivulets.

Three frogs perch
on the slick side of the rock.
I see them only now
that I am in noticing. They remind me
of those tiny ceramic frogs
I once coveted in roadside shops,
crossing country in the family
station wagon, me in the boot.

Completely still. So I become still, too,
not glass shelf still but in the glory of adsum.
Try to see what they see. Huge maple branch
spread low, mirroring itself in the shallow pond,
dipping its leaves in algae blooms,
sun tamping any shivers into place.

So many wings: swallows, dragonflies, wasps.
A clay-spotted lizard comes close, a butterfly lands.
I am a frog statue, a newborn lover
of the quiet pond. I name my mentors
Basho, Buson, and Issa,
masters in the distillation of beauty.
Together we sit and sit and sit.

The Creek

It was what we loved most about the land, hidden
by a massive wall of wild blackberries choaking

oaks and olive trees, suffocating spindly poplars,
boxes still unpacked, neighbors unmet, we spent unmasked

days tunneling through barbed brambles with gloved hands
and hearty cutters clearing a path to the creek. Its music

grew louder daily, cheering us on as we yanked tightly
wound tendrils, loosed young fig saplings from strangling

vines, and everything began to breathe a little easier.
We began a song down in the bed as we gently

removed packed leaves and twigs, to-go cups and chip
bags tossed from cars—the careless things of man clogging,

always clogging. Free now,
we let the creek run icily over our nicked fingers as it rushed

to run up against stone and root, mossy bank as if to say
I've missed you. How I've missed you.

To Love What Is Hidden

asks us to consider the cosmos
beneath our feet, to trod gingerly,
gently bend haunches,
lift leaf detritus,
expose the damp mess
in search of the simple mighty.
There, there, a life
bearing a calcareous shell,
a safely curled home
that now more than ever
we wish were our own.

I Am Snail

I move in slow, ever-widening circles
gathering in carefully sussed bits,
expanding out just a little
as my courage rises, taking tiny bites and
chewing them a hundred times each,
the bitter with the sweet. But the child
lost to a well's gaping mouth, three dead
fathers, miscarriages of justice and hoped-for
children, long-held power and fists of ego
escalating to guns poised at yet another border,
I cannot gather.
I retreat back into my spiral shell to digest
the darkness, winding myself into myself.
My great slick foot pulled in, one sucker pod
left out to test the temperature
of what's to come. Hoping, like all of us,
for a tender path.

Too Many Nights Now

I've carried her small pink shoe
searching for reason,
churning my mind
into all that urgently needs my worry,
my fear, my sadness. I turn sleep over
to what wrings my heart
of sense and joy, unable to distract the
busy clench of faceless strangers
with the rhythmic breath beside me. No wool
worth counting, no soft bell chiming,
no drifting with pills. My mind stays at war.
One foot escapes the sheets to sense the
cool air of my privilege. I eventually fall
with the weight of this large hurt
and all its unknown constellations.
And yet light comes and comes and
peels me from the ruin. The scent of pressed
oranges. One thin ray cast across the wooden floor.
An invitation I will accept again.

I Sit Here Waiting

for pleasurable words
to come for you. Something about the perfection
of plum blossoms or the scent of a just cut orange.
How music lives in trees and the sponge of moss
never holds a footprint. What comes instead is
the sting of shrapnel, ears cottoned by broken drums,
muffled cries in a language I don't understand.

Mercy.

How do we go from marmalade on toast
at the sunny kitchen table
to stuffing a duffle with what's in reach? How do we
leave it all behind, just go, and think what stayed—
now a shelled still life—
was a safe life just days ago?
Distance is the essence of my privilege.
Lives are falling. Lives are fighting.
There is resistance.
Here, the cherry blossoms are holding
in an unforgivable show of beauty.

Three Peace Nonets

Paradoxical Thinking

I am cradling two truths at once
gathered across the vast divide.
There is pain, there is beauty.
I am strong, and I weep.
Trees and people fall,
I plant more seeds.
They suffer,
so I
love.

Renewal

If I were a bee, I'd pollinate
all the dusty blooms in the field,
spread soporific love tales
of hope in the downpour,
tell the trees to sing
to the saplings,
newly sprung
from soft
ash.

When This Is All Over

Fall into each other's arms again.
Dance with the earth just as it is.
Put the phone down and breathe in.
Let your soles drink the ground.
Take in the wisdom
of an old tree.
Be a bird,
be a
bee.

Wheels

Don't you want to pull a red wagon behind you
full of all the things you love? Fill it up with familiar
comfort and take it with you down a pebbled path?
Books bumping the sides, dirty blanket,
a lunchbox of snacks,
a favorite doll left at the bus stop on a gray morning,
a lost doll returned in the mailbox by a kind stranger,
streaky face and dirty dress dampened by tears of relief
and disbelief. And I thank you, even now, for surviving
every day you were gone,
for making it home.
I wish I had that wagon now, wish I could resurrect
loved ones gone missing, fold them gently in the blanket.
Back in the wagon you go, and all is well with the world.
Wheels loosening gravel, rusty T bar in my hand
as I pull us all forward.

I Wake Knowing

the call will come saying you have gone.
I light a candle before I get out of bed
so the stars are kept company
for a few more minutes before the sun
obscures their ancient wisdom.
I say a prayer for you before the alarm sounds.
I know so little about life, although I am more
there than here. Only that the constants are few.
And not constant at all, more like puppets
pulled up the wall, dancing, miming shadows
of joy and pain, life and not life. I cannot say death.
I prefer continuation or maybe transformation.
I know you will stay around, my friend,
as a deep mystery. In the way the candle flame
pinched between my fingers sputters smoke—
a sweet, acrid reminder of its time as light.

A Mother in Your Absence

(for Sunny)

I sit very still
in the void of your leaving
and allow them to arrive one by one,
the whole committee of missing you.
I am flayed open to sadness, fear, self-doubt,
all armed with assumptions and judgments
and the searing truth of
what this parting has always known:
This is the nature of things.
I am not consoled by this jury,
so I straighten my back, zip my heart,
tuck my womb against my spine, lay a hand there.
This is only rain, I insist. *The cord is strong.*
With every worry comes a prayer, so I make my plea:
May yours be a tender path, as free of obstacles
as a life can be, the tripping full of kind lessons.
This is the only way I know how to be
a mother in your absence—to invite faith
to pull up a chair and hear me out,
to lean in close and whisper your name.

Metamorphosis

(for my mother)

Can you feel me? I'm right here, sitting on the yellow sofa.
I see you. The young you, this you, all you've ever been.
Time has accelerated the progress of loss
in the curve of your spine—gravity hanging your head, not shame.
The shapeless legs and swollen knees pinning you,
and all the while the brain remains lit and alive!
aware of the failing body, the parting breath.

In the quiet penumbra,
particles of you lift and settle on my lashes
like the ash of the night moth
just as I left cells in your womb
in exchange for ancestral wounds
and the history we never spoke of,
all mangled wings
spiralling along a line of DNA.

Through the simple connection of our hands,
gossamer skin and stubborn bone, we liberate each other,
forgive me
coursing from me to you and back again,
lifting us up and out like fireflies released
from a mason jar.

You are massive to me, even in your frailty. Massive
is my heart with this love-grief.

I am tethered still to life as you rise.
May you go easily in dreams,
the night full of ascension. Daylight
and you are home.

What to Take

My sister asks if there is anything I want before it all goes
to auction. Stacks of old framed photos, foxing around
the edges. All from a time I hardly remember her. Boxes
full of shoes too small, pants too short, facepowder
cracked and dry, just a shade too orange. Old tea in
tins. Bucolic landscapes framed in dust. The heat is on,
no one has bothered to turn it off. I pick up the beige
plastic watering can she kept in the corner and fill it,
water the dry ferns and the papery white orchid, the
variegated amaryllis someone sent her for Christmas,
growing instructions still attached. Three buds pushing
up through limp brown leaves on a single stalk, staked to
hold up all that still wanted to bloom.

still rooms left intact
as though someone might return
place in bright sunlight

Things That Rise

Yeasted bread, laments
voices in song
tides and egos and kites
veils and hems above vents
beat-down souls
most birds and buds
temperatures in August
lit paper lanterns and prayers
hot tempers of the unhealed
the rising agents of
worth
hope
joy
sun
weighed down by
old stories, untrue
strong arms and knives
lack of funds and fairness
skin color, class and
labels that were never ours,
and still
something pulls
and tugs
and bruisingly insists
that a soul in motion
stays in motion.
May it be you

the thing
that rises,
and knowing air
reach down
to lift
another.

Seeds

The song you send up
the words you pen
your thought, your prayer, your hope
once airborne
may land near someone, somewhere
with no voice
with nothing left to hold
no more room for belief,
and that soul you may never know
may tuck your seed into the recesses of their
halved hearts and let in this fertile thought:
Maybe, maybe I am not alone.

A Prayer

May you find splendor
in life's ordinary gifts—
grace of the goldfinch,
spider glory, mantis dance,
furl of tendrilled fiddleheads.
May the hidden and holy
invite you to life.
And too, I wish you a calm lake
on difficult days
full of everything you need.
May there also be
a skiff, oars, sunlight.

Japa Mala

Time weaves its way
between the years
a strand of offered pearls
I finger like a rosary
as blessing after blessing
solid in its sleave of prayer
must slip through and give way
to the next, thumbed
forward and forward
over mounds of grief and grace.
How large each moment feels when
we pause to feel its weight.
Formed from a single grain of sand
enveloped again and again
standing in for so much life
we count and hold and name.

Notes

"Marriage Tanka" and "Morning Tanka" follow the Japanese Tanka form of poetry consisting of five lines, with a syllabic count of 5,7,5,7,7

"Imperfect Buddha" and "What to Take" are both Haibun, a prosimetric Japanese form combining prose poetry and haiku, a three-line poem with a syllabic count of 5,7,5

"Birth Story" is an hourglass Nonet, a standard Nonet followed by a Reverse Nonet. See notes on both below. The form lent itself well to the themes of birth and how quickly our children seem to grow up.

"Poetry Ancestors" was inspired by a Master Class I took with former U.S. poet laureate Joy Harjo, where she spoke about the concept of poetry ancestors: those poets, dead or living, who profoundly influence our own poetry through style, form, beauty, and even borrowed lines. I included lines from her poem "She Had Some Horses" to illustrate her meaning and the freedom this concept offers to poets.

"The Faraway Nearby" with thoughts of Georgia O'Keeffe was created for a wonderful video exhibition curated by Sarah Fletcher entitled "Picture This Three Ways: Spaces and Places that Changed Me" featuring nineteen creatives in collaboration. Photographers inspiring writers whose poems then inspired visual artists. The project can be viewed on YouTube.

"Noticing" is a Burning Haibun, a poetic form invented by Torrin L. Greathouse, where the first part is a prose poem that then "erases" into a shorter poem, that further erases down to a haiku.

The title of "Crooked Hallelujah" was borrowed from the book of the same title by Kelli Jo Ford, although the subject of the poem has nothing to do with the book.

"Migration" is a Cascade Poem, a variable length form invented by Udit Bhatia where each line from the first stanza repeats as the final lines of each successive stanza.

"Transformation" follows a double form: The Golden Shovel, where each word from a line or lines are taken from another poet and used as the end word for each line in the new poem. In this case the last line of "Archilochus Colubris" by José A. Alcántara. It is also a Reverse Nonet, a nine-line poem with a descending syllable count beginning with one and ending with nine syllables.

"Three Peace Nonets" follow a nine-line descending syllable count, the first line beginning with nine syllables and ending with one.

Acknowledgments

My thanks and gratitude to the editors of the following journals, anthologies, and creative projects where these selected poems or previous versions of them first appeared:

Braided Way Magazine: "Dervish," "Rose Worthy," and "Paradoxical Thinking"

Hope is a Group Project Anthology, Wee Sparrow Poetry Press: "Things That Rise"

Humana Obscura: "What Branches Hold"

One Art: A Journal of Poetry: "Trip"

Picture This 3 Ways: Spaces and Places That Changed Me Video Project: "The Faraway Nearby"

Pink Panther Magazine: "A Memory of Kerala"

Quillkeepers Press/Rearing in the Rearview Anthology: "Daughter," "Birth Story," and "Wheels"

The Mindful Word: "Bray"

The Path to Kindness: Poems of Connection and Joy: "No Small Thing"

I would also like to thank the following people for saying "yes" when I asked and for their support, feedback, and encouragement:

James Crews, for his generous contributions to the poetry community and for writing such a beautiful introduction to this book. Donna Hilbert, Michael Kleber-Diggs, Laura Grace Weldon, and Laura Foley for taking time out of their busy schedules to read my manuscript and offer their blessings and commentaries. Amy Spaulding for her editing advice and keen instincts. Fernwood Press editor, Eric Muhr, and his competent team for their professionalism in producing these pages. The *Writing Beyond Your Comfort Zone* poets for their loving support and inspiration. The Beta Delts, both here and gone, for holding me throughout these many years. And to the many prompt providers, poem inspirers, pen wielders and word witches in the Instagram poetry community.

Last but not least, my gratitude and love to the wide, tangled net that is my family.

Title Index

W

First Line Index

www.ingramcontent.com/pod-product-compliance
Lightning Source LLC
Chambersburg PA
CBHW010857090426
42737CB00020B/3409